INDIGO MOODS

Alison M Lowther

www.green-cat.co

DEDICATION

I dedicate the works within this book to all of those who were involved in my past traumas, without whose influence I would have had a different journey and would not be the strong and resilient person that I am today.

I give thanks to my long-suffering partner Alan without whose unconditional love I would not have flown so high.

With much love and pride for my four beautiful children, Daniel, James, Bryan, Louise, my grandchildren and great grandchildren. Please know that you are truly my world, may you always find and know love in your hearts, and have the courage to follow your dreams.

.

Soul

I am soul,
And all I ever wanted
Was to be seen,
To be recognised,
I am here,
I am behind those eyes that you look into,
I am within that heart that you 'love',
I shine out to you,
But you are blind to my light
All you see is my body,
Yet here I am,
I am soul,
And all I ever wanted,
Was to be seen.

Part One

Those Emotions

Grief

In the deep, dark night
Through the long, lonely hours
As she wept inside
Her soul cried,
Her heart was torn
In a thousand pieces.
Her grief deep, wretched in its pain.
Her suffering immense,
Her feelings of helplessness overwhelmed her,
Deep down in her heart she knew,
Knew that he was by her side.
He was forever in her heart,
She was forever in his arms;
She felt him,
She knew always
That he would never leave her, not really.
His body, his body failed him
But his soul, his very essence, the realness of him
Lived on, always and forever
Eternal and never ending;
Infinite, just like her love for him
And his love for her,
Endless and infinite and always there, always felt.
Heartfelt,
Beautiful,

Pain and sorrow,
Love and warmth
Mixed in excruciating combinations of ecstasy and pain;
But the pain would fade
Eventually
She knew
But right now
She felt the pain
And his arms tight around her
Holding her close,
Comforting her,
Telling her
I am safe,
I am happy,
I am free of pain.
Do not cry for me,
Live your life
That is all I ask.
Be happy,
Be you, be the woman I love.
Do not change because of me
For I have not changed,
I am here still,
I am the same
Just not in pain;

<u>Rage</u>

The Rage,
That Rage
That burned,
Burned deep,
Deep inside her,
Deep in the very essence of her being.
That deep, burning Rage,
It threatened to engulf her,
To devour her,
To destroy her
If she would allow it,
She knew it was there;
Felt it.
Ignored it in the hope that it would go
Away
But it didn't,
No,
It just festered,
Ever deeper,
Ever more powerful;
All consuming.
Consuming her,
That Rage deep inside,
How it burned,
How it hurt her.
She knew she had to free it

But she did not know how;
So, she let it do its thing,
She let it roar,
Unleashing her anger at everyone and anyone,
At those she loved,
At those she loathed,
At anyone unfortunate enough to cross her path,
But she knew she could not carry on,
She knew the Rage would destroy her,
She knew she had to deal with it,
Knew she had to delve deep, deep into her very core
And wrench it out!
She tried
But she could not do it,
So, she decided instead to use it for good.
She harnessed the Rage,
And instead of allowing it to fester and hurt others
She became a warrior
And turned that Rage into a powerful positive force
To fight battles against the dark within her,
And so instead of being dark
The Rage was her weapon against the dark,
And so, it began;
The warrior was born.

Sadness

She wept,
Darkness wrapped its wings around her,
The night in its glory surrounded her,
Deep, dark and hungry it crept
All the while she lay and wept,
Wept for the losses,
Wept for the pains,
Wept for the anger,
That roared through her veins,
She knew she could,
She knew she would
One day defeat the rage within her,
But in this moment, it tore
And wrenched
Through her very soul,
Deep, dark and hungry it crept
As the night in its glory surrounded her,
And darkness wrapped its wings around her,
She wept.

Fear

Fear,
It traps you.
But it also keeps you safe.
Safe within your comfort zone.
For fear is a gate.
If the gate stays closed
And fear keeps hold
Nothing new can ever be found,
Only the frustrations of being stuck,
Of being limited,
Restricted.
When you open that gate
And walk through it,
Life will never be quite the same.
You will walk new territory,
You will face new challenges,
New experiences will open up before you
And you will embrace them.
You will be happy,
You will be free.
Free yourself.
Get marching through that gate like a boss.
Kick fear in the ass!
Stop existing,
It is time to LIVE!

Distrust

I haven't changed,
No not at all,
Perhaps
You never really knew me,
Perhaps it is that simple,
But I guess I never let you in,
Never truly trusted
that you would not hurt me,
that you would not leave me,
And so, you did,
And you did because
I didn't,
So, you see,
I am still the same,
Playing a game,
A game I can never win
If I don't let anyone in.

<u>Anxiety</u>

The rooms of the mind,
They are all entwined.
The sounds in the head
Filling them;

The noise and the voices,
Decisions and choices
Churning around
The mind.

Rooms filled with dread
Consuming the head.
Worry, anxiety,
Perpetual thought;

Plans and ideas,
Worries and fears
Fighting for a place,
Always competing.

If the mind would be hushed
And the thoughts unrushed,
The rooms would be tidy
And the head would clear.

Desire

Her heart pounded
Deep inside her chest.
Her soul cried,
Called,
Yearned
Behind the water in her eyes;
Hold me,
Love me,
Raw
Beautiful
Desire.

Dreamscape

In the mists of a dreamscape
I see your face,
The intensity of your eyes
Revealing the depth of your very soul
That stirs a yearning deep within my own soul
Like I never felt before.
Then I awaken
To another reality
And you are gone,
Why do I only see your face,
In the mists of a dreamscape?

Rejection

Just because I tell you something about myself,
Or because you judge by what I wear
Or how I look,
Just because someone said this or that about me
Or you judge by my lifestyle,
Just because I share my beliefs with you
Or you judge me by my opinions,
Does not mean that you know me,
You can never know me,
For I am constantly changing.
To truly know me
Is to connect with me
And that, my dear, you can never do.

<u>Real</u>

She was real,
She had temper,
She was wild,
Uninhibited,
Raw.
She was never one to hold back her feelings,
She expressed herself with a reckless abandon
That was either respected or feared;
She didn't care which.
She was raw,
Uninhibited.
She was wild,
She had temper,
She was real.

<u>Misunderstood</u>

You never understood me,
No-one does.
Oftentimes I never understood myself,
I closed the doors,
On you,
On everyone,
Oftentimes I closed them on myself.
To truly understand another
requires a knowledge, that can only be gained
By accessing the depths of the soul,
And this soul will not permit
Her depths to be accessed
So, you will never understand me,
No-one will.

Let it Go

Let it go,
You were not to know,
How could you know?
Do not blame yourself,
Never blame yourself
For having the most beautiful caring soul.
For hoping,
For loving,
For being you,
Never forget that you are a true angel
In a world of turmoil,
You are the calm,
Never blame yourself,
Do not blame yourself,
How could you know?
You were not to know,
Let it go.

Part Two

This Life

The Flow

The river flows
To where?
To the vast stretch of water that awaits,
To the mighty ocean beyond.
Stones may blight its path,
Rocks may alter its flow,
But nonetheless
It will continue
To flow on.
The river flows
Endlessly, tirelessly,
Knowing, trusting,
That no matter what obstacles are placed within its path
It will reach its destination,
It will arrive at where it is heading
Without doubt,
Just as you will arrive at your true destination
No matter what obstacles are placed in your path,
To challenge you
To test your faith,
By being like the river
And flowing with life
Whatever it throws your way,
You will reach your destination,
You will get to your chosen place,

Trust in yourself,
Believe in yourself,
Go with the flow,
Have faith in the universe,
For life flows.

Whispers

They spoke to her.
The trees,
Whispers,
Rustling,
The breeze taking the leaves
To flight,
Whirling down to the earth below.
Letting go,
Freely falling
Fearless without hesitation,
Dropping away,
Trusting
That they will land on the earth
And feed it,
Nurturing the soil,
Bringing new life,
The cycle of death
Bringing birth,
All in the simple act
Of letting go,
The cycle of life and death
They spoke to her.

Dawn

Walking by the river
In the early morning dew,
Her naked feet feeling the moist cool grass beneath,
Every step slow and purposeful,
She felt connected
To the earth below,
Felt the energy of the earth
In her feet,
Walking by the river
In the early morning mist,
She gazed across the water
At the trees,
Enveloped in wisps of misty cloud,
Green and moist
In summer's prime.
She looked to the horizon
Where the sun was beginning to rise
Over the sea ahead,
Breaking through the mist,
Preparing for a new day
Bringing light and warmth,
And she gave thanks and gratitude
For another day.

Mirrors

Life is full of mirrors,
They are all around you,
Everyone you meet
Is a mirror,
A reflection of you,
Whether you know this, or you don't
It is so.
The universe shows you who you are, and what you
need to do.
She shows you the way
Through the reflections of your soul
Within the others;
The others whom you distance yourself from,
Because you cannot tolerate their company,
Because you feel discord toward them,
Because you do not 'like' them.
This is so
Because they are reflecting,
They are mirroring something
That lies deep within you;
Deep within your psyche
That you do not like about yourself
And so, you do not like them,
You do not like what they show you,
But if you do not face it

And you do not acknowledge it
Then it will always be there
And then it will always be reflected,
And so, you will keep meeting others
Who will reflect it
Until you see it
And you say, "Ah,"
And you learn
And you face it
And you heal it,
And then and only then you will move forward
Another step in the game.
The game of life.

Love Heals

She was the light to his dark,
The yin to his yang.
She illuminated the demons within him,
And in doing so
She saw her own demons
Reflected,
Mirrored
In him
From her.
And only then
When fully exposed
Could they begin to overcome
Their problems, and exorcise
Their demons
Together,
This was love,
This was how love worked its magic,
Love heals
All.

<u>In the Blink of an Eye</u>

When you blink,
It makes you think,
That what you see is all that is there.
But stop a while,
Stop and stare,
And see through the veil,
At what is there.
What surrounds you are not the things
That you see, hear, taste, touch and smell with your physical
senses.
They are but one percent of all that is there.
The rest in-between is seldom seen
By the human eye,
Which will only see
What the brain will allow.
Know this, believe this.
There is much around you that you cannot see.
There is much to life that you can be,
If you would only believe
In what you cannot see.
It is all just a game,
A virtual playground.
Your body an avatar,
Your mind a computer.
Switched on or switched off?
Well that all depends on you,
And on what you believe to be true.

Redemption

Redemption is
What?
Redemption of sorrow, trust, thoughts, worries and
anger?
Redeeming the wrongs to permit the rights?
But what is wrong and what is right?
Definition gets in the way.
Always.
Always in the way,
Defining this and defining that.
All the while analysing.
Why, and to what end?
To label, to define, to put in a particular box, to fit, fit in.
But you were born to be different.
Everyone is different, individual.
So, fuck the box.
Fuck fitting in.
And fuck redemption!

Tick Tock

Mindless morons walk the street
Shuffling along,
Their feet
taking them
Ignorant, asleep, in deep, dark slumbers
Oblivious to the truth,
Brainwashed by media,
Educated to conform,
To only believe.
What they see with their physical eyes.
What they hear with their physical ears,
Oblivious to the truth that walks alongside them,
But they do not hear
For they have no desire to,
They have a comfort that comes with ignorance,
For ignorance is bliss, is it not?
So, on they walk,
And when they reach home, they switch on their televisions
And believe all the lies before them,
Like mindless zombies they soak it in,
Try telling them that they are lost
Try waking them up to the truth.
They will do what they are programmed to do.
They will laugh and call you crazy,
Ha, if they could only see
How crazy they have come to be
And the world they are living in,
Wakey wakey
Tick tock tick tock tick tock

<u>Night and Day</u>

He was her sun,
She his moon,
He was day,
She was night,
Opposites,
Complementing,
Reflecting,
Balancing,
Yin and yang,
Light and dark,
Night and day.

<u>Now</u>

There is no yesterday.
There is no tomorrow.
There is not even today – all there truly is, is now.
This moment, the now.
There is not time.
So why waste what you don't have thinking about a day
that is not in existence.
Smell the coffee.
Taste the air.
Hear the birds sing.
See the beauty around you.
Feel the love.
Stop thinking and start living.

<u>Nature</u>

Nature is my chapel,
My place of peace and healing,
Deep into the woods I go to ease my weary mind,
Deep into the healing roots that surround me
And soothe my very soul.
The energy of the trees,
Their colour, their softness
Surrounds me,
Grounds my body,
Soothes my emotions,
Reminds me of my own roots,
My true home,
My true birthplace
From where I came
And to where I will go,
One day,
When I leave this world and return,
Home.

The Raven

Black as night,
Shining bright
Feathers
Glistening in the moonlight.

Black eyes
Under dark moody skies
Peering out,
Watching,

He watches and waits,
Perched on the gates
Of his kingdom.
Protector.

The gate between realms
Guarding the helms
Of the ship
Of dreams.

Part Three

Those
Inner Demons

<u>Shadows</u>

Shadows,
Blackened fleeting glimpses
Gleaned from the corner of her eye.
A solitary shadow
In the night
Facing her, facing it,
Her darkest edge,
Her deepest fears,
Displayed in front of her,
Showing her,
Her shadow,
Her shadow side,

She kept it down,
Throughout the day,
Kept it hidden
Out of the way,
But when darkness fell
Through the long, hard night,
Always there was,
The fight;
Fighting with herself,
With her demons,
Her darkness,
Her shadows.

<u>Mother?</u>

Who are you?
Do you know?
I mean, do you know who you really are?
Oh, sure you know your name,
You may be lucky enough to know your family,
Perhaps you even have the privilege of knowing your
roots,
But I ask again,
Do you know who you truly are?
I think not,
For you do not have any knowledge of the missing link;
Your firstborn!
One day you may awaken
And know your loss.

Sanity

Sanity sits,
Perched on the edge
Of the conscious mind,
When thoughts are good
No matter what comes up against it
Sanity keeps its hold,
Stays perched – on the edge,
When thoughts go bad
And all hope is lost,
The smallest pressure
It comes against
Will push it
Over
The edge,
To where conscious and unconscious meet.
To uncertainty,
To confusion
It loses its place
It falls,
Deep,
Into insanity.

<u>Depths</u>

She crawled through the depths of her mind,
Swerving between the shadows in her path,
Void of vision, void of sound, void of taste,
Void of smell, void of feeling.
Empty, searching
Through the darkness she wandered
Aimlessly,
And when dawn broke
She rose and went about her day,
Void of her senses.
Robotic, she functioned
Until night fell,
And she crawled through the depths
Of her dark shadow-infested mind.

Wait Till Your Father Gets Home!

'Wait till your father
Gets home,' Mother said,
Those words tore right through me
Filling me with dread,

What did I do?
I did nothing wrong,
Am I really so bad?
What have I done?

I heard the key turn
In the lock of the door,
My stomach turned over
I stared at the floor,

His footsteps approaching
A sound filled with dread,
He strode through the hallway
My feet turned to lead,

'She's been a bad girl today,
Talking back.'
My father's hands
Reached for the rack,

The rack where he kept
The belt, thick and wide,
'Bend over girl,
I'll belt your cheeky hide!'

I bent over the chair arm
As I always had to do,
And he lashed at my legs
Till they stung red and blue,

He carried me to my room,
Carried me by the neck,
He threw me down and slammed the door
Shouting, 'What the heck!'

Then Mother said to Father,
'Now that 'that's' out of the way,
Would you like a cup of tea?'
'Oh, and how was your day?'

<u>Bad Girl</u>

'Please Mummy no!'
'Mummy no, please don't go.'
'Stop Mummy, stop!'
'Please Mummy, no!'
She stood on the landing
At the top of the stair,
Screaming and screaming
As her mother descended
The long winding stairway.
'You're a bad girl!' she shouted,
'I'm going away!
And when your father returns
You can tell him
That I have gone away,
And it is all your fault!
It's your fault I am leaving
Because you are a bad, wicked girl!'
'No!' she screamed, 'No!'
'Please Mummy no!'
Daddy would belt her,
Daddy would hate her,
Daddy would hurt her,
It was all her fault.
And mummy was leaving her,
Again,

Her other mummy left her,
Her other mummy didn't want her,
Now this mummy didn't want her either,
Nobody wanted her
Because she was bad;
Bad and wicked,
That's what they said,
A bad girl.
So, she would be belted
And her daddy would not want her either,
She screamed
And screamed
And screamed
Till she could scream no more,
Then she lay on the ground
And sobbed.

Lost

She always knew she was different,
She never fitted in
And never really wanted to,
She never belonged,
Never complied,
Never really understood
why those around her lied;
Lied to themselves,
Faked their ways,
She never shared their humour,
Or their views
And their beliefs.
Neither did she pretend to,
For it didn't feel right,
Didn't feel real,
She never felt like she belonged,
All she ever wanted
Was to return
Home.

Noise

Echoes all around;
Sounds,
Noises,
Voices,
Outside, in her ears,
Inside in her head,
Noise, disturbance,
Black noise, white noise
Consuming the void of an empty mind
That could not bear
To remember.

<u>Denial</u>

Something is not right,
You know this,
But you fill your head with stuff
In avoidance,
You clean
In avoidance,
You cook
In avoidance,
You do stuff for others
In avoidance,
You will continually obsess and busy yourself,
Just to avoid the knowing,
That something is not right.

Part Four

The Epiphany

<u>Epiphany</u>

Her heart was sore,
It hurt,
Tight, binding,
Restricting her,
Her breath was laboured,
Her chest was tight,
The air would not flow
It could not get through,
For she had built a fortress
Around her heart,
A wall of steel
To keep at bay
Anyone who tried to love her.
She feared rejection,
Feared being let down;
Again,
Abandoned;
Again,
But then she realised,
She was all she needed,
She was enough,
She would love herself,
Love herself so fiercely that she would do whatever she
desired to do,
Be who she desired to be

And then her heart would be free.
If someone else would love her,
And someone else would leave her,
Then so what?
Would it really matter?
After all she had herself,
Loved herself,
And it was all a matter of perception
She realised,
They were not rejecting her,
They were not abandoning her,
They were projecting onto her,
Their own fears,
Their own insecurities,
It was never about her,
It never had been,
It was always about them,
And that epiphany
Set her soul free.

<u>Warrior</u>

She had had enough of hurts,
Enough of disappointments,
Of fears,
Of the biased opinions of others.
She would go her own way,
She would walk her own path.
She was borne of all she had suffered,
Carved of all she had endured,
And she would use the pain
To propel her motivation,
To fuel her determination,
To put fire in her soul
And passion in her heart,
She would walk her own path,
She would heed the voice of her own heart
And the gentle whispers of her own soul,
She was a warrior reborn
And she would fight her ego
And slay her demons.
No more would they dictate her life,
She made a choice,
To be herself
Unashamedly, unequivocally
Her true self,
Real,

Raw,
Wild and rebellious,
She knew who she was
And what she wanted,
No longer would she exist,
Now she would start to live!

Light

Her soul sank down
Into the dark night,
Long and deep
It swallowed her,
Consumed her,
Drowned her in its deep, dark embrace.
She could have allowed it to take her,
But she remembered
That where there is darkness there has to be light
So, she fought and found that tiny spark within her
And embraced it,
And it grew, then she shone it
And made her way out
To a dawn that was brighter than any she had ever
known
Now she was truly free.

Into the Arms of Love

She crawled through the depths
Of despair and desolation
Searching for something
But not knowing what.
A way out,
Solace
To escape the never-ending labyrinth of despondency
To which she had fallen
So desperately.
Then she felt it – his touch,
Heard his voice,
Knew his name.
His name was love,
And he was calling her.
She crawled through the depths
And into the arms
Of love.

The Conqueror

How she had suffered,
She had endured the pain,
The trauma, the relentless kicking of her very soul,
But she stood strong, she fought back,
Then she turned around and strode away,
With all the power and passion of that wild woman deep
inside her,
She conquered her demons
And moved swiftly on,
Liberated, free,
Now she could move on,
Now she would create the life she wanted,
The life she would love.

<u>The Battle</u>

The battle raged inside her,
One she could not win.
She had erected her defences,
Put up her walls
To keep them out,
Keep them away
But in doing so
She had imprisoned herself,
Trapped herself
Within her own walls.
Her defences were also her jail,
And on it raged
Until the pain could be borne no more,
She knew she had to surrender;
Surrender to others,
Surrender to life,
Allow them in,
Permit the love
And whatever they would bring,
She was strong after all,
She could handle it,
She would deal with it,
Anything was better than this torture she had created for herself,
So, she let down her defences,
Took down her walls,
And in freeing her heart
She herself was free,
Free to be herself
And she knew
She would be,
She could be
Happy.

Freedom

The opinions of others
Mattered not to her,
She made her own music
From deep within her heart,
She danced to her own beat
From deep within her soul,
She lived her truth,
She walked her own path,
Caring not for wearing shoes made by others
For feet that were made to feel the earth.

A Warrior Made

No one is born a warrior
For a warrior is made,
With a dose of trauma,
A few handfuls of suffering,
A selection of beatings and kicks,
Knock downs and knock backs,
From which she rises
Stronger, tougher
Resilient,
With a new-found passion
To never allow more
For her or for anyone,
And a new warrior is made,
A warrior with purpose.

<u>Found</u>

In the deep, dark rooms of her mind
She roamed,
Lost and alone,
Confused and forlorn.
Not quite understanding
Just what was wrong.
Something not right
But she just could not quite
Grasp what it was – until,
She saw the light;
A glimmer at first
But she saw it, and she grasped it, and she shone it
for the world to see and her heart to feel,
She glowed, she shone,
Now she was real.

Broken Wings

She had grown tired of repairing the broken wings of
fallen angels,
Weary of stitching up the hearts of the torn.
She woke up and realised
It was not about their broken wings,
It was not about their tears,
They were her mirrors,
They were reflecting to her, her own broken wings,
Her own tears,
Which she had denied and avoided
By fixing them in others.
Finally, she mended her own tears,
Repaired her own wings,
And she flew.

Wild Woman

She knew she had done something that was not good for
her when her stomach churned,
Her inner voice screamed at her,
But she did not listen, had chosen not to hear
For her mind did not like what her heart was telling her,
It made her ego insecure.
So, she had ignored it,
And now it welled up inside her,
That wild wanting,
The desire to be more and to do more,
For too long her wild woman had slept
But now she had awoken and would succumb no more,
Now they would hear her roar.

The Way-shower

She adored long candlelit baths
On a cold winter's evening.
She liked nothing better than to sit by the window
On a cold but sunny day,
Sipping tea and watching the birds play.
She loved to dance, and she did so every day with
reckless abandon!
She was happy in her own company,
She appreciated what little she had
And her gratitude warmed the universe,
And because she was truly happy
Her inner light shone showing others the way.

Roar

Her soul screamed,
Screamed deep inside her
But she did not listen,
Did not hear it
Although she felt it,
She ignored the screams,
Dissed the voice inside,
Until she could bear it no more,
So she let it out
And allowed it to roar.

.

<u>Roots</u>

Her roots were weak,
Fragile,
Loose,
She swayed,
She rocked
And she stumbled,
Then she fell.
She lay and she wallowed in the tight embrace of self-
pity,
Then – she picked herself up,
Dusted herself down
And dug her feet in deep,
She would stand steady,
She would stand firm,
Rooted, strong and tall,
Up she rose; a warrior born
Never again to fall.

This Journey

This journey was hers,
She would do as she pleased,
She would go where she wished,
She belonged to no-one,
Answered only to herself.
For too long she had bent to the will of others,
Had gone where she was led.
No more would she bend,
No more would she follow,
She knew what she wanted,
She would go where she wished,
She would do as she pleased,
This journey was hers.

Inner Child

Find the child that you once were,
Allow her out to play,
Embrace that innocence,
Remember that joy,
Wonder at the simple things,
Feel the freedom of simply being alive,
Acknowledge that bad ass within
The rebel that you were.
She never left you and has been waiting all this time,
Let her out, set her free,
Go get what you want, what she has always wanted,
Feel the freedom
Of following your heart
Of being in the moment;
Carefree and happy
Like a child.

Happiness

Through the deep, dark rooms of her mind
She roamed,
Searching through never ending shadows,
Peering through darkness,
Void of feeling,
Trapped in her mind
She was blinded.
Then she felt it,
That tug, that wrench deep down inside her;
In her heart, her soul
It called to her,
Something within her shifted.
She shifted,
From her head to her heart
And she realised
That was where it was
That thing she sought,
The Happiness.

<u>Letting Go</u>

Always on her guard
Analysing them,
Were they being honest?
Were they hiding something?
Could they be trusted?
It was hard work,
Took all her energy,
Made her sick
So she let it go,
Let go of the need to analyse
And trusted her intuition instead.
After all it was never wrong
So, she listened to it,
Trusted it
And her life began to flow.

Resolution

One morning she woke up feeling mediocre
With no desire to rise,
She felt sad and dejected,
Torn and neglected,
Not for the first time.
She was tired of that feeling,
Tired of feeling tired,
She made a resolution that never again would she feel
that way,
So, she got herself up,
Dressed in her best,
Looked in her mirror and said,
'I will not lie down,
I will sort this mess.'
And she did,
She made a choice there and then,
She stopped existing and started to live.

Mist

Strolling through the mists
Of a muddled mind,
Trying to make sense of it all,
Wandering lost and alone,
Trying to find her way,
Dreams come and go
But this .... This was real
And the mist failed to lift
A veil on her world,
Until,
She found that light,
And shone that light,
Her light,
That light that was truly her
And as the mist evaporated
She shone!

Scars

She had scars,
On her face,
On her body,
She was cracked,
Not broken.
No, she was stronger than ever,
She loved her scars
For they told a story;
Her story
Of battles won
Of a warrior born.

Lionheart

She heard a distant scream
Echoing from far away,
A heart-wrenching sound
That made her shudder.
It got louder
And closer
Until;
It was right there
Inside her head,
Not a distant scream
But her own.
She paused,
As from deep within her a lioness emerged
And she roared!

ABOUT THE AUTHOR

Alison identifies with the term Indigo Child aka Indigo. (One who is empathic, and strong willed with a sense of purpose and spiritual awareness. One who feels different and struggles to 'fit in').

Like most people, Alison has experienced her share of trauma and battles along life's journey. Having struggled with relationships and found the idiosyncrasies of society difficult to comprehend, Alison has used writing as a means of expressing her deeper feelings and frustrations, which she was unable to express verbally.

Currently Alison is a Reiki Master healer and teacher, psychic counsellor and empowerment coach, in her own small business. Within her healing role she has always used positive quotes and verses to inspire and empower people. Through her love of writing and of poetry she has compiled many of her own. Alison believes strongly that we each create our own reality and through her work she aspires to empower people to find and follow their own truth.

For details of our other books, or to submit your own manuscript please visit

www.green-cat.co